Helping

Your New Employee Succeed

Helping
Your New Employee Succeed

Tips for Managers of New College Graduates

Elwood F. Holton III
Sharon S. Naquin

BK

BERRETT-KOEHLER PUBLISHERS, INC.
San Francisco

Berrett-Koehler Publishers, Inc.
450 Sansome Street, Suite 1200
San Francisco, CA 94111-3320
Tel: (415) 288-0260   Fax: (415) 362-2515   www.bkconnection.com

ORDERING INFORMATION

Quantity Sales. Special discounts are available on quantity purchases by corporations, associations, and others. For details, contact the "Special Sales Department" at the Berrett-Koehler address above.

Individual Sales. Berrett-Koehler publications are available through most bookstores. They can also be ordered direct from Berrett-Koehler: Tel: (800) 929-2929; Fax: (802) 864-7626; www.bkconnection.com

Orders for college textbook/course adoption use. Please contact Berrett-Koehler: Tel: (800) 929-2929; Fax: (802) 864-7626.

Orders by U.S. trade bookstores and wholesalers. Please contact Publishers Group West, 1700 Fourth Street, Berkeley, CA 94710. Tel: (510) 528-1444; Fax: (510) 528-3444.

Printed in the United States of America

Printed on acid-free and recycled paper that is composed of 85% recovered fiber, including 15% postconsumer waste.

Library of Congress Cataloging-in-Publication Data

Holton, Ed, 1957–
  Helping your new employee succeed: tips for managers of new college graduates / Elwood F. Holton III, Sharon S. Naquin.
      p. cm.
    ISBN 1-58376-168-3
  1. Supervision of employees. 2. College graduates—Employment.
I. Naquin, Sharon S. II. Title.
    HF5549.12 .H65 2000
      658.3'0084'2—dc21

                                    00-011218

First Edition

05 04 03 02 01 00   10 9 8 7 6 5 4 3 2 1

Cover and Interior Design: Bookwrights Design
Editorial Services: PeopleSpeak
Indexing: Directions Unlimited

To our parents:

Ed and Betty Holton
and
Jim and Marjorie Smith

Contents

Preface

A large part of our professional careers is devoted to management and leadership development. One of the great ironies we have observed is that few management development training programs or degree programs include much information about how to develop new employees. Yet one of the key tasks *every* manager and supervisor will have throughout their careers is to bring new employees into their organizations and develop those employees. And the research is clear that what occurs in the new employee stage has direct effects on employee productivity and retention. We don't understand why such an important stage has been overlooked, so we decided to do something about it.

This book addresses one very frustrating new employee situation managers face—bringing new college graduates into their organizations. In every organization in which we have worked and interviewed people, mentioning new college graduates as new employees elicits groans and comments that they just aren't ready for the work world. Managers are convinced that colleges aren't doing their job and young people aren't as mature these days. They lament the fact that they lose many talented new college graduates as employees. The funny thing is, the new college graduates are just as frustrated! So what is going on?

It turns out that both new college graduates and their managers "don't know what they don't know." As you will see in this book, colleges do not teach students how to make the transition to work. Worse yet, they actually countertrain students because the process of succeeding in college is so different from succeeding at work. If you are managing new graduates and don't understand this dynamic, you are destined to make mistakes and be frustrated as you try to develop them as employees. The good news is that this book will show you how to do it right.

Over the past twelve years we have used the twelve-step process described in this book to coach countless new employees on how to make a better start in their careers. Our challenge in this book was to package our advice in a concise, user-friendly format so readers could quickly learn the system in today's hurry-up world. We know this system works and you can use it to avoid a lot of frustration, help new college graduates become productive quicker, and keep your talented new hires. A little learning can make a big difference in your new employee development.

Preface

Our sincere wish is that this book will help you do a better job with your new employees as you help them make a successful start in their careers. Good luck.

Elwood F. Holton III
Sharon S. Naquin
Baton Rouge, Louisiana

One

Getting the Most from Your New Employees

Congratulations! Your efforts to recruit and hire an excellent new employee have paid off. You've reviewed piles of resumes and interviewed countless applicants. The job candidate of your choice, a new college graduate, has accepted your offer and is eager to report to work. Both you and your new employee have high hopes for a successful relationship and are excited about the possibilities. But how can you be sure that your newly hired employee will make a valuable contribution to your organization? Can you do anything to increase the likelihood of a successful employee-employer relationship? Conversely, can either what you do or what you fail to do during the first few months contribute to a decrease in the productivity or effectiveness of your new employee? The answer is an emphatic *yes!*

A well-designed and well-executed employee development program is essential to help reduce turnover and improve productivity. New employee development is a tremendously underutilized strategic tool that should be a central element in managing your company's human resources. When properly used, this tool will speed your new employees to maximum productivity and help ensure that you end up with the high-performing employees you really want.

But you have an orientation program or process, you say? That's terrific, but it's only a start. Even if you have the best training program in the world to teach new employees how to perform their job tasks, you're *probably* still far short of having a complete new employee development system.

The Complete New Employee Development System

Effective new employee development extends far beyond the traditional task-related training on which many organizations focus. Our intent is not to demean the importance of task training, but how many new employees have you hired who actually lacked the basic skills or raw talent necessary to perform their job tasks? Unless you are very new at hiring employees, your answer is likely "very few" because you know how to assess job applicants' basic skills. The fact is, more new employees will fail because of nontask-related problems.

In workshops with managers of new college graduates, we always ask participants to think of two new employees they have supervised: one whom they consider to be outstanding and representative of the type of employee that they would like more of and another whom they consider to be average. We then ask the managers to list the characteristics that differenti-

2

ate the outstanding new employee from the average one. Invariably, skills to perform basic job tasks either are not mentioned or are ranked very low.

To understand what is high on the list, imagine for a moment that you are a brand new employee of your organization. What would you really need to know to be successful in the first year? Of course, you would need some training in how to perform the specific tasks of your job. But you'd also need to know exactly what would be expected of you while you performed those tasks. You'd have to "learn the ropes" so that you would know how work usually gets done around the organization. You'd need to learn the politics of the office and get to know your coworkers' likes, dislikes, and pet peeves. You'd need to understand the culture of the organization so you could "fit in" and become part of it. You would need to get to know your boss well, particularly how to "read" him or her and do your job the way he or she wants it to be done. And all the while you would be trying to cope with the anxieties, confusion, and stress of being a newcomer. These are the items that are high on the list of characteristics that differentiate outstanding new employees from average ones.

Now ask yourself, "How could a new employee learn everything he or she needs to know? Is the information written down?" Not likely. Does someone take the time to sit down regularly with new employees to discuss these issues? Probably not. Are you pointing new employees in the right direction so they can learn important information quickly and independently? Possibly, but probably not very often. If your company is like most, new employee development is hit-and-miss at best once orientation is complete. Experience shows that a deliberate plan needs to be in place to help new employees learn *everything* that they need to know and become fully accepted members of the team as quickly as possible. If you don't have such a plan, you are losing money and your new employees are quickly losing motivation.

The Manager's Role in the Breaking-in Stage

The first year on a new job represents a separate and distinct career stage that we call the "breaking-in stage." The breaking-in stage is a unique transition period for *both* the individual *and* the organization. It requires both parties to use special strategies to be successful. Research has shown that the first year on the job is crucial for both parties. For the individual, what happens in the first year has a significant impact on salary, advancement, and internal job mobility. A new graduate's successful transition from college to work helps pave the way for more opportunities for success. This is called the "success spiral," and it is what new employees should strive for. For the organization, what happens in the first year has a major impact on the employee's commitment, satisfaction, and productivity, and, of course, on turnover. Neither party can afford to ignore this. The good news is that you can address this transition by adjusting your employee development program. The required changes won't cost you much but can yield enormous returns very quickly.

Still, few managers have ever been trained in how to bring a new employee into an organization, and few individuals have ever learned how to enter an organization successfully. A common result is often a year of frustration and disappointment for managers and new employees or, at best, a stressful and challenging transition period. It's no wonder then that the managers and new employees we interviewed have lots of frustrations, complaints, and wishes for a better way to develop new employees.

New employee development is the responsibility of everyone in an organization. One of the worst mistakes that can happen is for managers and others to see new employee development as "just a human resources function." Everything from employee development strategy to actual training needs to be a coordinated effort involving a new employee's manager, the human resources director, upper management, and others. In small companies, these roles may be filled by only one or two individuals, but in large companies they may involve many people. Whatever the case, as a manager of new employees, it is your job to make sure that effective development efforts occur. You therefore need to understand the overall strategy as well as the specific actions you need to take. After all, it is you who will be affected most if the new employee's productivity suffers. This book is therefore written from a broad perspective so you will understand everything that needs to occur, even if you will involve others to help you.

How to "Lose Your Shirt" on New Employees and Not Even Realize It

Are your new employees as productive as you would like them to be? Do they seem to take too long to become an effective part of the organization? Are you losing too many new employees after you've spent lots of money to hire and train them? Does it seem like your new employees are struggling more than they should? If the answer to any of these questions is yes, then your new employee development system is probably costing you money.

As you are undoubtedly aware, hiring new employees is costly for any organization. The cost of recruiting can quickly add up, and the selection and interview process often consumes countless hours of expensive management time. Add to that the cost of training new employees, the cost of their inevitable mistakes, and the cost of their lower productivity as they move up the learning curve, and you'll quickly realize that you have an enormous investment in every new employee you bring into your organization. The rule of thumb is that the cost of hiring a new employee is *at least* equivalent to the employee's first-year salary and is usually higher.

It's amazing then to see how little many organizations do to protect their investment. Many organizations—large and small—invest considerable resources in hiring the right people and in managing their performance and advancement but leave most of the new employee development process to chance. If your organization is one of them, you could be losing large amounts of money. Even worse, you'll probably never know it because most of the costs aren't directly visible on your income statement or in your budget. And the more new employees you hire, the greater the cost to your organization. Moreover, your accountant, controller, banker, or anyone else will never notice!

Ask yourself how much time you've actually spent planning each new employee's entry into your organization. Time is precious, but would you spend as much money on a new piece of equipment as you have on one year of an employee's salary without carefully considering how to get a good return on that investment? Probably not, so why do it with new employees?

Two

Building Blocks for New Employee Success

The New Employee Development Process

Employee orientation and development programs serve a variety of purposes both for the new employee and for the organization. They help

- welcome new employees

- communicate to new employees that they are valued within the organization

- foster positive impressions about the organization

- validate employees' decision to join the organization

- provide basic organizational information to employees

- assist new employees in understanding their job responsibilities and managers' expectations of them

- communicate performance standards

- provide a basis for training and help assimilate employees into the organizational culture

If these programs are executed well, turnover rates decline, morale improves, training costs are reduced, employee satisfaction rises, and productivity and work performance improve. In short, the results are mutually beneficial to new employees and to the organization as a whole.

However, successful employee development programs are not a one-time event. It's impossible for new employees to learn everything necessary for success in just a few days of orientation. Said differently, a successful employee development program extends well past providing a tour of the facilities, conducting a few days of speeches by management, and distributing policy manuals. An effective employee development program has these key elements:

- It is an ongoing and structured process.

- It begins with a job candidate's acceptance of a job offer, not on the first day of work.

- It involves dialogue and interaction with all levels of the organization.

- It is viewed as extending throughout the first year of employment.

- It includes goals for nontask as well as task performance.

- It teaches the new employee, the manager, and the new employee's colleagues how to collaborate for a successful first year.

- It is a priority for the organization.

College Is a Different World

Hiring new college graduates can bring fresh energy, ideas, and enthusiasm to your organization. It can also bring frustration as these employees adjust to the world of work. You probably know that college is a unique and special world—but you won't realize *how* different it is until you have new graduates start to work for you. At the heart of the problems most new graduates (and their managers) experience during their transition is the failure to recognize how much the educational culture has shaped their attitudes, expectations, behaviors, and overall view of the organizations for which they choose to work. Think about it. College graduates have spent at least seventeen years in education. How could they not be shaped by their experiences?

Ready for a big surprise? College is so fundamentally different from work that not only does it leave new graduates inadequately prepared for work, it countertrains them! That's right. It makes it *harder* for them to adjust to work. The *knowledge* they acquired will be critical to their success in your organization, but the *process* of succeeding in school is so different from the process of succeeding at work that they will struggle to make the adjustment. Worse yet, the culture of education is so different from that of the workplace that if they have the same expectations of your organization and you that they did of their college and professors, they'll be greatly disappointed with their jobs, make costly career mistakes, and frustrate you greatly. By taking the time to teach them the culture of work and what it means to be a professional, you'll help them avoid making fools of themselves by taking classroom behavior into the workplace.

These are some of the key differences that new graduates talk about:

COLLEGE	FIRST YEAR OF WORK
Frequent, quick, and concrete feedback (grades, etc.)	Infrequent and less precise feedback
Highly structured curriculum and programs with lots of direction	Highly unstructured environment and tasks with little direction
Few significant changes	Frequent and unexpected changes
Flexible schedule	Structured schedule
Frequent breaks and time off	Limited time off
Personal control over time, classes, interests	Need to respond to others' directions and interests
Intellectual challenge	Organizational and people challenges
Choice of performance level ("A," "B," etc.)	"A"-level work always required
Focus on personal development and growth	Focus on getting results for the organization
Opportunity to create and explore knowledge	Expectation to get results with one's knowledge
Individual effort	Team effort
"Right" answers	Few "right" answers
Independence of ideas and thinking	"Do it the company's way"
Professors	Bosses
Less initiative required	Lots of initiative required

Notice that the culture of college is opposite that of work. However, new graduates usually don't know what they don't know. When we conduct workshops with new graduates after they've been on the job about six months, most of their complaints stem from the fact that work is not like the left-hand column—but they don't realize this until we show them this comparison table.

Let's look at a few examples of how failing to recognize this big culture change can have an adverse effect on new graduates in the workplace. College provides concrete direction about what is expected. Students are given syllabi for courses, standards by which their work will be graded, curriculum guides plotting four (or more) years of study, and so on. If students happen to have a professor who is less structured in terms of a course syllabus or grading criteria, chances are they will complain—loudly. At work, new graduates rarely get the type of direction they're accustomed to, so they may well complain that their bosses won't tell them what to do.

Have you ever thought that new graduates are argumentative? Think about how their college education taught them how to argue a position to convince a professor that they were right and the professor was wrong. Did you ever think they want too much feedback and seem insecure? Think about how accustomed they are to being frequently told "how they're doing" (e.g., via grades). Do your new hires seem like they want to attend training seminars too often or demand too much new learning? Think about how accustomed they are to growing and developing through education. Do they seem impatient with work that is more routine or mundane? Think about how college stretched their minds.

You and your new employees will have many misunderstandings if you're not careful. If you do what comes naturally, you will become impatient with them because they act like college students. If they do what comes naturally, they will do what they've done for seventeen years—act like students. Even more frustrating is the fact that the best students are the ones who will struggle the most with the transition because they were good at performing in the college culture.

You must realize that almost no college is doing enough to teach students that the "rules" will change dramatically when they go to work. You bear the brunt of this problem. We have found that 80 to 90 percent of managers' and new college graduates' complaints are either caused by or greatly exacerbated by their failure to recognize the deeply ingrained differences in attitudes, expectations, and behaviors between college and work. And it is this misunderstanding that can cause new graduates to be labeled "naive" and "immature," cause them to be frustrated, and cause you to lose valuable new employees.

First-Year Goals

The goals of a new employee development system should specifically include socialization (i.e., helping your new employees learn about the organization and how to fit in), as well as training in task performance, and should be integrated with other human resource processes. Equally important as achieving productivity is helping your new hires achieve three other objectives: earning acceptance, earning respect, and earning credibility. You should help them understand that becoming an outstanding employee requires much more than technical skill or know-how. They need to realize that no matter how brilliant they are or how successful they were in college, it is nearly impossible for them to receive an outstanding performance rating at the end of their first year without first mastering the nontask aspects of their jobs.

New graduates are likely to have a fundamental misunderstanding about what is really important in the first year on the job. Most will probably think a lot about the tasks they've been hired to do. They naturally assume that they will finally have a chance to put their long years of study to actual use. They see many exciting opportunities to develop and showcase their abilities as they tackle new challenges. They may also be a bit insecure, a bit worried, and anxious about their abilities. What they don't realize is that most employers are *not* worried about their ability to do their job tasks but rather their ability to do the nontask components of their jobs. New graduates need to understand that great performance on the basic tasks of their jobs will earn them only an average performance rating.

The conclusion: most new graduates are focused on the wrong details—task-related knowledge and skills. Why? Because these are what college focuses on. Your job is to help your new employees understand the full range of learning needed to become successful. Remember, most of them don't know what they don't know. The twelve steps outlined below will guide you in helping them focus on the nontask elements of their jobs.

Twelve Strategic Steps to Helping New Employees Succeed

Let's turn our attention to what new employees need to learn and how you facilitate their learning process. The following discussion focuses on a twelve-step model that portrays the key developmental tasks for new employees. This model is based on extensive research and has been field-tested in organizations such as J. P. Morgan, Enterprise Rent-A-Car, the U.S. Department of Energy, the U.S. General Services Administration, and the Multiple Sclerosis Society.[1] The twelve steps are grouped into four categories, as listed below:

Individual Focus

Step 1: Foster the right attitudes.

Step 2: Manage new employees' expectations.

Step 3: Cultivate breaking-in skills.

People Focus

Step 4: Teach impression management skills.

Step 5: Help new employees build effective relationships.

Step 6: Help new employees become good followers.

Organization Focus

Step 7: Help new employees understand your organizational culture.

Step 8: Help new employees adapt to the organizational system.

Step 9: Help your new employees understand their roles.

---

[1]Elwood F. Holton III, "Preparing Students for Life beyond the Classroom," *The Senior Year Experience: Facilitating Integration, Reflection, Closure, and Transition,* ed. J. Gardner and G. van der Vere (San Francisco: Jossey-Bass, 1997), 95–115; and Elwood F. Holton III, "New Employee Development: A Review and Reconceptualization," *Human Resource Development Quarterly* 7 (1996): 6–10.

Work Task Focus

Step 10: Help new employees develop work smarts.

Step 11: Help new employees master the tasks of their jobs.

Step 12: Help new employees acquire the necessary knowledge, skills, and abilities.

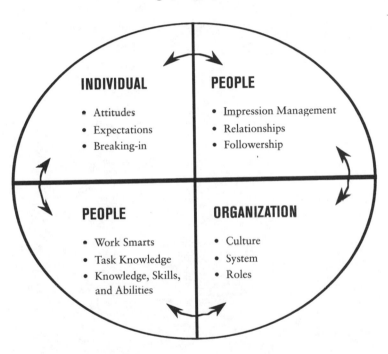

Figure 1 illustrates the model. The following chapters elaborate on each of the twelve steps in the new employee development process.

Three

Step 1: Foster the Right Attitudes

The chief complaint voiced by employers is that new college graduates don't bring the right attitudes to the workplace. Perhaps you have expressed this same criticism of new employees yourself. You can help alleviate this problem by identifying and communicating "success-related attitudes." More specifically, teach your new employees which attitudes will enable them to succeed within your organization.

To do this, identify the people in the organization who are viewed (both by you and your superiors) as successful. Note their attitudes toward their supervisors and colleagues, their jobs, the organization, and the future of the organization, and communicate to your new hires the success-related attitudes and values these people have. Commend these individuals for their exemplary attitudes and encourage others to use them as role models. On the flip side, take time to identify attitudes that are viewed as inappropriate. Confront individuals with these inappropriate attitudes and explain the probable consequences.

Here are some key attitudes and characteristics that managers in almost every organization say new graduates need to develop:

Humility

New employees, particularly new college graduates, often arrive at the workplace with a false sense of their importance and capability. They frequently make the mistake of thinking that their successful college careers will effortlessly translate to successful professional careers. In fact, it's quite common for past campus leaders or academic standouts to struggle the most with the transition from college to the working world. This mistake is understandable given that the very characteristics that helped them excel in school are typically what attracted you as an employer to them in the first place. And countless other organizations have probably been beating down their doors to recruit them, too. After all, what prospective employer isn't excited about signing on the college overachiever? Thus, the graduates' pride in their accomplishments and their confidence are justifiable, but they can get in the way of success. Your job as a manager is to help your new employees balance their self-confidence and sense of self-importance with the realities of the world of work.

Readiness to learn

Encourage learning among your new employees. Let them know that you value their willingness to learn even more than you value what they already know. Provide ample learning opportunities for your new employees and encourage their participation. When work is slow around the office, provide your new employees with additional training, something to study, or an opportunity to participate in new projects. If they express an interest or show enthusiasm for a new project, take note and offer additional training. As a manager, you should recognize and encourage passion for work projects. When possible, you should allow your new employees to pursue new ideas or projects and reward their efforts.

Readiness for change

If your organization is like most, a flexible and adaptive attitude wins points. Yet new graduates often lack this valued characteristic. Organizational life is full of changes, and new graduates need to be flexible. However, colleges are designed to resist change, whereas business organizations try to respond to change. As new hires, college graduates frequently complain that the world of work isn't what they expected. You should be prepared for this reaction among your new graduates and plan strategies to foster their readiness for change.

One such strategy focuses on encouraging your new hires to routinely reevaluate their progress. Have they made and achieved their personal short-term goals or remained stagnant in their roles as a newcomer? Are they developing to their fullest potential as employees? A second strategy involves trends. What are the current trends within your industry and your organization? How does your organization plan to meet the demands associated with the changes that are occurring? How do you expect your employees to meet these demands? Discuss these issues with your new hires and help them alter their course of action to meet the changing demands of your work environment.

Respect

Implicitly, every employer expects respect from individual employees—respect for himself or herself as a manager and respect for the organization. New employees sometimes must grapple with the fact that their new boss or organization isn't perfect. Yet they must understand and appreciate that both their manager and their organization are the way they are and work the way they do for some reason. No managers or organizations are perfect, but new employees must respect them for what they are. As a manager, you can help foster this respect in new employees in two ways: by showing respect for your new employees and by helping them better understand the "whys." Remember the Golden Rule learned in childhood: Treat others as you would have them treat you.

Helping employees understand the "whys" is very important in fostering mutual respect between employee and employer. All too often, decisions are made or actions taken that may seem illogical, unreasonable, or unwarranted to new employees. Many times, this perception (or misperception) stems from the fact that new employees have not been privy to information considered in the decision-making process or do not understand the nuances of the situation. When confidential information is not involved and you are at liberty to share relevant facts with your employees, do so. Not only will they feel a sense of inclusion, they will feel respected. In turn, their respect for you and the organization will grow.

Confidence

New employees know that their employers want to see confidence. After all, their confidence in their abilities helped them sell themselves in job interviews. They may not be aware, however, that their confidence might look like cockiness to others. You want the right kind of confidence among your new employees. What will earn your respect is confidence about their potential combined with humility about their newness and lack of organizational savvy. Teach this to your new hires. Help temper their pride in their previous accomplishments with a sense of realism about their current situation. What they can achieve now may not even resemble what they have achieved in the past. Tell them that nobody jumps right into a job knowing everything necessary to succeed and you don't expect them to be the exception. Allow your new employees to demonstrate a capacity to *become* competent in their jobs rather than expecting them to be competent immediately.

Open-mindedness

Few managers want new employees who have preconceived notions about what work ought to be like, how it ought to be done, and what employees are supposed to do. You probably prefer that your new employees start with an open mind about the organization and its way of doing business. It's doubtful that you want an employee who is a "yes-person" or a blind follower, simply accepting your organization's methods and practices. But you also want your new employees to try your ways of thinking and working before they attempt to change them. You want them to be open to your organization's ways of thinking and working.

You can help cultivate open-mindedness among your new employees by encouraging new ideas and sharing the organization's history and the evolution of work methods and processes. Explain why what you do is appropriate and necessary. Let the employees know that their thoughts and ideas are welcome, but they have to learn the way things are before they can talk about the way things could be.

Long-term perspective

Employers typically view the development of new employees as occurring over several years, not just a few months. New graduates, on the other hand, have become conditioned to courses that last from just six to fifteen weeks. A successful professional's attitude is one that says, "What I'm doing today or even this month is not as important as where the work may take me down the road." This is the perspective that you should foster among your new hires. You want them to willingly accept assignments that may not be fun but are good training, to accept assignments that may not be exciting or glamorous, and to stay focused on long-term goals. Unfortunately, they have become accustomed to shorter time perspectives.

How can you change their outlook in their first year on the job? One way is through communication, which is a key factor in laying the foundation for their future. Discuss possible career paths and development activities. Explain the relationship among the various work processes within your organization. Let them know how what may seemingly be the most menial of tasks fits in the overall organizational picture. Remember that successful employees understand the purpose and direction of their organization and how they can help the organization reach its goals.

Work ethic

Most graduates consider themselves to be hard workers. After all, they've successfully endured the rigors of college life. Yet many graduates soon find that professional life is a lot more demanding than college. Accordingly, employers often complain that graduates aren't ready to work hard to meet those demands. They are often disappointed when new graduates fail to show up early, stay late, volunteer for projects, and work extra hard at learning.

You can help your new hires go that "extra mile" and do whatever is asked, no matter how trivial it may seem. The most obvious way to do this is by example. What type of work ethic do you and other managers within your organization exhibit? What you do and say gets noticed and sets an example for your new employees. If you are routinely late, you are communicating that being on time isn't important. If you routinely violate the formal policies and procedures of your organization, you are telling your employees that policy and procedural compliance isn't a priority. Your actions demonstrate your standards. Perhaps even more important, what type of feedback is given to new employees regarding their work ethic? Because new employees want to make a good impression, your feedback may be your most powerful tool for fostering a strong work ethic among your new hires.

Positive attitude

College students often complain about their professors, "dumb" assignments, the slow and bureaucratic administration, or the workload. This isn't the attitude you want in your workplace, yet many new graduates continue the habit of complaining. You want to see a positive attitude and not hear whining or griping from your employees. Let your new hires know that complaining is discouraged, even though older employees may do it. You can discourage complaints and negative attitudes by showing your own enthusiasm for work. Your willingness to work and your eagerness to accept new responsibilities can be contagious among your new employees. You can also provide feedback to your new employees that tells them a positive attitude will get them much farther than a negative one.

Points for Reflection

Think for a minute about the people in your organization you consider successful and whom you would like new employees to emulate. What attitudes do these people exhibit that have helped them be successful? These are the success-related attitudes in your organization.

What are you doing to teach new employees these attitudes or at least teach them which attitudes will be rewarded? When you think about previous new hires, which attitudes were they least likely to exhibit naturally? What are you doing to focus development efforts on teaching these particular attitudes? How should you change your new employee development and coaching programs to do a better job in this area?

Four

Step 2: Manage New Employees' Expectations

Unmet expectations are a major cause of the frustration many new graduates experience in their first jobs. Frustration is nothing more than the difference between expectations and reality. As a manager of new graduates, you can help them avoid disappointment by providing a realistic picture of what they can expect early on. Don't let them feel as if walking into the workplace every day is like walking into the middle of a mystery novel or suspense movie because they never know what's ahead. Help them know what to expect by roughly mapping out their routes for the next year. Discuss the specifics of their job descriptions and the performance standards by which their efforts will be measured.

Also be aware that your organization's recruiter (or maybe even you) may have painted a picture of your organization that was a bit too rosy. Similarly, during the interview process, you probably lavished attention on prospective employees in your eagerness to convince them that your organization was the right place to begin their professional careers. But now that they are on your payroll, the situation has changed. The pressures of your own deadlines prevent you from devoting a lot of time and attention to your new employees. Furthermore, even if you had an abundance of time, you didn't hire these new graduates to hold their hands and walk them through every step of their first year on the job. But you can't afford to ignore them, either.

Remember our earlier discussion about the major differences between college and work? These differences create many unrealistic expectations. They also make it very important for you to make time for your new employees. Sit down with your new employees and clearly explain the specific duties and responsibilities of their jobs and what is expected. Ensure that they have a clear understanding of what behavior is tied to their future compensation and opportunities for advancement. Show an interest in them and provide feedback on their progress. You can also conduct realism audits to examine pre-employment activities (i.e., are you presenting an accurate picture of your organization or painting a rosy picture?), monitor new employees for expectation-related frustrations, clarify expectations and correct inappropriate ones, provide experiences to reinforce proper expectations, and anticipate disappointments and replace them with new goals. Remember, experienced employees know much of what the organization expects of them without ever needing to be told. It's easy for managers to assume that new employees understand far more than they really do. New employees, who are anxious to impress, often hate to ask.

Points for Reflection

Think about new college graduates who either left your organization within the first year of employment or had a hard time adjusting. Now think about the frustrations they had and the complaints they may have voiced. Is there any pattern to them? How might these frustrations have represented unrealistic expectations? Similarly, how might your frustrations with new employees represent improper expectations that have not been properly dealt with? What can you do to clarify and correct employees' expectations so these frustrations might be prevented?

Five

Step 3: Cultivate Breaking-in Skills

Your new hires must realize that there is a different set of guidelines to follow now that they've entered the work-force. As you help them cultivate breaking-in skills, you will see that your job is twofold. First, you must help your new hires learn a few inescapable facts about their first year on the job. (Astute newcomers will do this on their own.) Second, you must help them cope with the rules that correspond to these facts.

The following are the guidelines they need to be aware of during the breaking-in period.

New hires are outsiders until they prove otherwise

Just because your new hires are on the payroll doesn't mean that the people in the organization have accepted them.

Acceptance of newcomers from your existing staff isn't automatic; it must be earned.

New hires are unable to change the system until they become a part of it

When insiders criticize the organization or attempt to make changes, it is considered constructive. However, when an outsider such as a new hire criticizes or suggests changes, this probably will be viewed as an attack. The presumption is that until employees know the organization well and are a part of it, they can't possibly understand procedures well enough to make constructive criticisms.

"Big splash" strategies aren't always best

It's normal for new hires to want to impress you and their new colleagues by showing how smart and talented they are. This strategy, however, backfires when implemented before the new employee has taken the time to understand the organization and has earned acceptance from its members. Rather than impressing others, they usually end up embarrassing themselves. Therefore, the quickest way for a new hire to make a "big splash" is to have the maturity not to try.

For new hires, admitting what they don't know is more important than showing what they do know

Recognizing how much there is to learn within a new organization is critical for new hires. Before they can make a positive impression, make intelligent suggestions for change, or have new ideas accepted, they must learn as much as possible about their new company and its employees. They need to "learn the ropes" and to understand the nuances of how business is done. New hires must realize that what makes the most positive impression is not showing how much they know but rather having the maturity to know how much they don't know.

Conformance may be more important than individuality

Organizations typically do not value or reward individuality—especially in their new hires. A certain level of conformity is expected. For instance, it's highly unlikely that a conservative bank's newly hired management trainee would earn points by showing up for work on the first day with a pierced eyebrow and tongue. On the other hand, an Internet company consisting mostly of Gen-Xers may not even give that look a second thought. In order to gain acceptance during the breaking-in stage, new employees must demonstrate some conformance to the established rules, norms, and methodologies of the organization rather than challenging the system. Initially, they must work to fit in; otherwise they will run the risk of looking like an immature new graduate. In time, newcomers will have plenty of opportunities to develop their own style and assert their individuality.

Newcomers have to build a track record

The old saying is true: Nothing sells like success. New hires should look for opportunities to be successful and should strive to become known for their dependability, willingness to work, adaptability, and professional maturity. This will help them get on the "success spiral" quickly. They should be careful to make the right mistakes—that is, those that come naturally from learning, not those that come from immaturity and impatience.

Unquestionably, these are hard lessons for most new hires, but you can help. Teach your new employees the breaking-in skills they will need. Clearly identify development milestones, and have ways to teach informal organizational learning skills. Help them fit in and provide opportunities for them to develop their own styles, assert some individuality, and make their jobs fit better. More important, provide opportunities for successes—even small ones.

Points for Reflection

Each organization is a bit different from others, but all have certain norms about how a new hire can be accepted quickly by other people in the organization. Most of the time these norms are unwritten, so some new employees learn them, and some do not. Think back to the time when you were new with your organization (or talk to someone who was new recently). What key actions did you take to be accepted? What makes people accept new employees as part of the team instead of treated as an outsider? Are you teaching new employees these strategies?

Six

Step 4: Teach Impression Management Skills

The old adage about never getting a second chance to make a first impression holds true in employment situations. And, at the risk of piling cliché on top of cliché, this "works both ways." Thus, both you, as the manager, and the new employee must make a concerted effort to make a good impression on each other. It can't be emphasized enough that if you are to retain your employees, it's critical for you and your organization to make a positive impression on them. So roll out the red carpet and let them know that they are valued and appreciated. Make time for them and do everything you can to reduce their uneasiness. Take pride in their work so that they will too.

Your new employees need to realize that everything they do early on will be magnified in its impact. In addition, it's hard to define precisely what the "right" impression is since every organization is different. That's why the new hires' first challenge in making a good impression is having the professional maturity to figure out what the organization wants to see. Chances are, this will be a difficult feat for them. Here's where you can help. Coach your new employees on how to manage impressions. You can also partner your new hires with a positive role model who can provide examples of good impressions. Ideally, this should be a "seasoned" employee who knows the organizational ropes; has a good performance history; is compatible with the new employee in terms of age, education, and so on; and has good interpersonal skills.

Another strategy for teaching impression management skills involves bringing the "success spiral" to life and teaching your new hires about it. The "success spiral" is an upward spiraling course that emerges as the responsibilities of new employees broaden. You can help your new employees by creating opportunities for them to be noticed, to have better opportunities, and to build on successes. You can also reward positive impressions and encourage other employees to minimize judgments based on first impressions.

Points for Reflection

If you were picking a team of new employees from different departments in your organization to work on a project, which employees would you pick? What did these new employees do that made you notice them and think they might be good to have on your project? Do other managers notice the same actions? Are your new employees being taught that these actions make a positive impression? Conversely, what did the new employees do that made you not select them for your team? Are new employees taught that these actions make a negative impression?

Seven

Step 5: Help New Employees Build Effective Relationships

The importance of effective relationships should not be minimized or overlooked. The ideal work scenario for your new hires is not one in which they are isolated in their offices, working long hours to complete assigned projects, taking manuals and books home to learn more, skipping lunch to make sure the work is done just right. Working in isolation like this does not promote effective new employee development.

Organizations aren't just collections of tasks and duties but are people working together to achieve a common goal. People shape an organization, determine how work gets done, decide employees' futures, and determine the success of the organization. In addition, the only way new employees will learn how to become successful in an organization (how to accomplish goals, what the culture is, how to sell their ideas, and so on) is from other people within the organization. These lessons are not written down and can be learned only from others within the organization. It then follows that building good relationships is the only way that they can be successful in their jobs. Without strong relationships within the organization, your new hires will not develop into outstanding performers.

Here are some suggestions for helping your employees build effective relationships:

Create opportunities to build good working relationships

The most obvious way to help your new employees build good working relationships is to provide opportunities for them to develop relationships with as many people as possible and to set goals for your new employees that require relationship building. You must make time available for relationship building and identify critical relationship networks for new employees (i.e., relationships with colleagues who will be influential in their success). Design activities that facilitate building key relationships, and include new hires in activities and projects that force them out of their offices and into groups. Where appropriate, assign new hires to committees and task forces. Encourage and reward teamwork. Introduce new employees to others and invite them to lunch. These simple acts can help break the ice for the introverts and provide just the occasion that an extrovert may need to cultivate strong work relationships.

Help new employees understand what good working relationships are

New graduates may not understand that you don't have to become social friends to be good colleagues. Work relationships are different from personal relationships. Your new hires have become accustomed to associating with people who like them on a personal level. But as you know, this isn't always possible in work situations. Teach your new hires the differences between work colleagues and social companions.

Provide opportunities for new employees to develop good communication and relationship-building skills

Your new employees should learn to communicate and work well with all types of people. They must also learn how to negotiate differences, how to avoid or manage conflict, and how to see others' perspectives. Examples of these skills as applied in your own workplace can be a valuable teaching tool. By example, teach new employees to respect and work with all types of people. If necessary, you can also provide opportunities for your employees to participate in interpersonal-skill-building programs.

Encourage new employees to network

The old saying is true: Who you know is just as important as what you know. Help your new hires build a network of contacts, resources, advisers, and sources of information. You can accomplish this by identifying and providing support relationships within your organization and by making certain that your new hires are in regular contact with strong role models. Encourage your experienced employees to make regular efforts to include new employees in their networks. Persuade your new employees to take advantage of opportunities to attend social functions, meetings, or seminars where they can meet colleagues, even if they must do it on their "own time."

Points for Reflection

List at least five groups of people who you think will be particularly important to your new employees' success in their new jobs. What steps should new employees take to build good relationships with these groups? What are you doing to facilitate the process? Are you taking the time needed for these relationships to emerge? Be sure to consider peers, support staff, other members of your work group, resource networks, senior management, and other groups.

Eight

Step 6: Help New Employees Become Good Followers

Without a doubt, you are the most important person in a new hire's first job. As a manager, you are in a position to

- provide opportunities to showcase the talents of new hires

- see that they get the necessary training

- set the tone of their first year

- shape the organization's opinion and evaluation of them

- determine any advancement beyond the entry position

- socialize your new employees to the organization's culture

Accordingly, you should help build positive and mutually productive relationships with your new hires. This is as much your responsibility as it is your employees'.

Unfortunately, college courses aren't designed to teach employees how to be effective subordinates. Just as there is a well-defined set of skills you learned to be a manager, so too is there a well-defined set of skills for subordinates. Colleges focus on developing future leaders, but becoming a good leader requires first learning to be a good follower. Therefore, you should clearly and concretely discuss your expectations with new employees as well as strategies for getting ahead. You must define effective followership skills for your new employees and coach them in their efforts to develop these skills.

Here are some key pieces of information you need to share with your new employees so they can build good followership skills and be effective subordinates:

- How much information you like to have

- Whether you like to get regular updates or just know about problems

- Whether you like to be offered solutions to problems or be part of the problem-solving process

- What your standards are for quality work

- What your agenda is—your wants, needs, and expectations

- How your new employees can best support you

- How hard you expect your new employees to work

- What the key demands are on your time

- What critical resources your new employees can help obtain or conserve

- How your new employees can help you be more efficient and productive

- When you need your new employees to be most available

- How your new employees can become indispensable to you

You also need your new hires to become easy employees to manage. Focus on the following:

- Which decisions you like to make and which ones you will delegate

- The way you are most comfortable giving feedback

- Areas in which it is particularly important that your new employees stay flexible

- The level of job ownership you prefer to see exhibited

- The degree of independence you like in new employees

- The manner in which your new employees should express disagreement

- The best way to get help from you if it is needed

- What your new employees should do to exceed your expectations when you make a request or give instructions

- The best way to respond when you give an assignment

You can also foster followership skills by providing opportunities for your new employees to work closely with subordinates you consider to be effective. Their example to your new hires will reinforce the information you have provided and help to elicit similar behavior from your new hires.

Points for Reflection

Every boss has his or her own style, quirks, and needs. Because of this, new employees often have a hard time learning to adjust to a new boss. Here's how you can help:

1. Make a list of what new employees can do to make themselves *indispensable* to you.

2. Make a list of your "hot buttons"—that is, actions employees take that are sure to annoy you.

3. Make a list of what new employees must absolutely do for you to help you get your job done.

4. Now, meet with your new employees and share these lists.

Nine

Step 7: Help New Employees Understand Your Organizational Culture

Every company has an organizational culture that is simply the "personality" of the organization or the rules and norms that shape everything that occurs within the organization—from the way individuals interact to the dress code. Some people refer to organizational culture as the "around-hereisms" that you hear every day: "We don't do things like that around here" or "We like to see people working hard around here."

Some of the critical elements of organizational culture include

- the mission and guiding philosophies of the organization

- basic values, norms, and behavioral expectations

- the work ethic

- what gets rewarded

- social norms

- management philosophies

- ethical standards

- sacred beliefs and events

- the general atmosphere and attitudes of employees

- communication norms

- work norms

In other words, the culture defines how employees do what they were hired to do and what's "normal" in the organization. Whether or not new hires realize it, they bought into both a set of tasks and responsibilities and a way of life when they accepted their jobs. How well they come to understand this way of life will have a major impact on their success in the first year.

There are two basic rules to remember about culture. First, organizations want employees who "fit" their culture and enthusiastically embrace it. It's highly unlikely that you and the other members of management within your organization want a staff of clones, regardless of how effective or productive any single organizational member may be. But, undoubtedly, there are limits to the level of individuality that is allowed within your organization. Second, employees aren't allowed to deviate from the culture until they are accepted as part of the team and have a track record of proven performance. That won't happen within the first year, so employees must focus on "fitting in." If they fail to understand the culture, they are almost assured of making many dumb and embarrassing mistakes that will hurt their careers.

Lack of knowledge about the culture of your organization may make your new hires feel insecure in their dealings with both their peers and their superiors. You can play a key role in assisting your new employees in their attempts to adapt to your organization's culture and overcome their feelings of being an outsider. First, you should define and clearly communicate the key elements of the culture. Translate this information into usable, everyday terms. Emphasize the basic mission and philosophy of the organization to your new employees. Clearly articulate what's expected of your new hires, particularly the accepted work ethic and social norms. Let your new hires know what's "right" and what's "wrong" within your organization. Knowing what's acceptable will help them more accurately interpret the reactions and responses that they get from other organizational members. And because levels of acceptability can vary by title and position, it's important for these cultural items to be defined for all levels of the organization. Use both experiential and cognitive methods to teach your new hires about your organization's culture. Finally, find some way (regardless of how small) to recognize or reward behaviors that "fit" within your culture (e.g., compliments, perks).

Points for Reflection

Your new employees probably considered many different employers before they chose to work for your organization. If you had to tell a group of college seniors what distinguishes your organization from others, what would you say? What is it about your culture that makes your organization different? That makes it effective? That makes it a good place to work? What do members of your culture value the most? Reward the most? Reject the most? Are you teaching your new employees all of this?

Ten

Step 8: Help New Employees Adapt to the Organizational System

As new employees adapt to an organizational system (the ways in which an organization really functions), they must recognize that politics plays a role in everything that happens within the organization. But the negative connotation that is normally associated with organizational politics does not necessarily represent reality. Politics is just the way things get done when people work together. It can be nasty and vicious but usually is not. Politics is the process of sharing resources, sharing power, and influencing others.

How can you teach your new employees to be adept in handling the politics of your organization? Begin by clearly communicating both "around-hereisms" and the dynamics of the informal organization structure. Take time to teach your new hires about the organization's power and political structure and to demystify how work "really gets done" within your organization. Identify the key "players" within the organization and the battles that are worth fighting. Explain what the controversial political positions are and the consequences of treading on this dangerous ground, and provide training in negotiating, if at all possible.

Not only are organizations political, but they are often illogical, are sometimes unfair, make the wrong decisions, are slow to do things, don't always welcome change, aren't always fun, and sometimes don't like newcomers. Not all people in organizations are nice, helpful, or motivated. Simply put, they aren't perfect. Your new hires may have pictured your organization as an ideal place during the interview process, but your organization's warts and blemishes will quickly be revealed. You should help your new employees accept and adjust to these realities. Begin by discussing these faults openly, but point out that it's possible—even probable—for them to be happy and successful.

Organizations establish elaborate formal structures, systems, and procedures, but the people in them develop their own informal structures and methods that are the way work really gets done. These are the "backdoor" ways of getting information, the shortcuts around the cumbersome accounting system, the informal agreements among departments to make work flow quicker. Thousands of procedures are never documented and simply evolve over time. Informal, unwritten ways of doing things make organizations more productive. Help your new hires master these methods so that they can achieve better results in their jobs. Clue them in on the meanings of the buzzwords and acronyms used within the organization so that they don't feel as if people are speaking a foreign language.

Show them the ropes. Keep them from getting lost in the "official" procedures, and point out "how things really get done around here."

Points for Reflection

Suppose you were writing a book called "Everything You Always Wanted to Know about How Work *Really* Gets Done around Here—but Were Afraid to Tell" and you knew your boss would never see it. What would you say about the politics of the organization? What would you say about how work really gets done? What would you tell people to help them decipher the unwritten rules of the organization? Now, go teach all of this to your new employees.

Eleven

Step 9: Help New Employees Understand Their Roles

The newcomer role within an organization can feel awkward. Think back to your first day at your present organization. Do you remember feeling frustrated and uncomfortable? Chances are, those memories are still pretty vivid. Your new employees are probably experiencing those same feelings (and possibly even having second thoughts about joining your organization). However, you can help them cope with their newness. First, explain employees' roles and how they fit into the overall organizational picture. Then, let your new employees know how their jobs affect the organization's bottom line, and help them understand what they are expected to accomplish in their first year of employment.

It's quite natural for new employees to develop "tunnel vision" regarding their new roles. They focus on their own needs, interests, and jobs rather than recognizing the big picture within their organizations. When assigned a "menial" task, such as copying documents or proofreading a final report to meet the deadline for a big project, they see it as "grunt work" instead of their part in helping the department complete an important project. If you don't have much time to talk with them for a few weeks, they feel neglected instead of realizing that many other very important matters require your attention. And if colleagues don't take the time to help new employees complete their tasks, the new employees feel shortchanged instead of volunteering to help with these other important priorities. However, if you arm them with knowledge of the "bigger picture," your new hires will view their roles as something more than "just a job." Rather than simply filling hours, they will feel a sense of purpose and direction and take pride in making a contribution to the organization as a whole.

In order for new employees to understand their roles in the overall scheme, it's essential for them to understand the company's mission and goals. Provide a broad introduction into the larger organization by including different parts of the organization in your employee development process. Explain how task assignments fit in the bigger organizational picture, and tell your new hires what they can expect in their new roles. Help them realize that their work outputs are someone else's inputs so they will understand how their work relates to other parts of the organization. Don't overlook the importance of clearly communicating when their roles are changing.

Every organization has certain tasks that new employees are saddled with. These are commonly called "rites of passage" or "paying your dues." In many organizations, because new hires are often the "low people on the totem pole," they must do copying, filing, or running errands. Sometimes they are assigned all the grunt work on a project and often get the worst desk and office (or cubicle). Some organizations won't allow new employees to write their own memos or take the lead in a presentation until they've worked there for a while. Let your new employees know that they shouldn't take this treatment personally. Sometimes it happens as a little bit of hazing and sometimes it's just because someone has to do the routine work. Everyone, including you when you were a new employee, has had to undergo such treatment. Regardless, you should discourage and minimize employee hazing as much as you possibly can. Help your employees to relax, and let them know that their opportunities will come.

Don't overlook another valuable resource available for helping your new hires understand their roles: experiences of previous new employees. Make these experiences available to teach and reinforce correct new employee roles. For instance, you can share stories of previous new hires' successes and failures in their efforts to understand and adapt to their new roles. How were the employees who successfully grasped their roles recognized? Were they rewarded? What were the consequences involved in the failures? Discussions centering on these issues will have a great impact on the ability of your new hires to understand their new organizational roles.

Points for Reflection

As illustrated in this book, new employees often have the wrong idea about what they should accomplish in their first year on the job. Managers, on the other hand, usually take it for granted that new graduates understand what is really expected of them. What exactly do you expect from your new employees in their first year? How will you judge if they have had a successful first year? What process have you put in place to clearly communicate this to them? To reinforce it throughout the first year? To let them know whether they are being successful?

Twelve

Step 10: Help New Employees Develop Work Smarts

S o far, you've considered your new employees' attitudes and expectations and helped them break in, build relationships, and understand the organization and how to work within it to get results. Helping your new employees develop "work smarts" is the next step in the process of helping your new employees become outstanding performers.

Here are two areas in which you can provide assistance:

Applying knowledge

While new graduates may have accumulated a wealth of knowledge during their college careers, the practical application of that information may be much more difficult than they ever imagined. Many new graduates comment that they struggle to apply the textbook information that they've learned to a job setting. To be an effective manager of new graduates, you should find ways to help them learn how to utilize their prior experience and expertise as much as possible.

Developing professional skills

Your new graduates will need to develop numerous professional skills in order to perform their jobs. These include

- managing time efficiently

- setting priorities

- juggling multiple projects

- writing memos, letters, and reports

- making oral presentations

- managing work flow

- managing and participating in meetings

- selling ideas

- projecting a good image on the telephone

- working with a secretary

- organizing work and your office

- setting realistic deadlines

- meeting deadlines

- producing the right level of quality

- motivating oneself

Focus on helping your new employees develop these essential professional work skills. Offer opportunities to develop and enhance these skills. Conduct performance reviews at least twice during the first year to give your new employees prompt and honest feedback.

Points for Reflection

As an accomplished professional, you probably take most of these skills for granted because they now come naturally to you. Unfortunately, that means you are prone to overlook the fact that many new graduates still need to learn them. Walk around your organization and talk to new employees informally. Ask them what skills college did not give them that they feel they need to get their work done. But before you do, resolve that you will not scoff at anything they say, even if it seems simplistic to you. What did they tell you? Were you surprised? Now, ensure that they receive training to build those skills.

Thirteen

Step 11: Help New Employees Master the Tasks of Their Jobs

While the emphasis in this book has been on the nontask elements of any job, task performance is also essential. After you take the first ten steps, your new employees will be able to really master the tasks of their jobs. Not only will they fully understand these tasks, but they will also understand how they fit into the organization, how work really gets done, and whom to work with to accomplish the organization's goals.

Here are three ways to help new employees become proficient workers:

Provide challenging work

Every employee wants to feel a sense of fulfillment in his or her job. New employees are no different. Yet all too often, new employees aren't given what they consider to be meaningful work assignments. While this is partly a function of the "breaking-in" process, you can find ways to alleviate the frustration associated with it. First and foremost, don't start by assigning your new employees seemingly endless piles of paper and manuals for them to read. This feels like insignificant busywork to your new hires and a way for you to simply "get them out of your hair." Assignments such as observing other workers and mastering your computer system, while often serving much the same purpose as reading manuals, seem more legitimate to your new employees. Your new hires feel more like they are part of the work process and less like they have simply been dismissed.

As your new graduates progress in their jobs, you should continue to provide work assignments with appropriate levels of challenge. Be proactive in determining these levels. Check employees' progress on past assignments and gauge their potential for success on increasingly challenging assignments. Don't forget to explain the purpose of assignments so that you can enable new employees to feel as if they are making worthwhile contributions to the organization. It's also imperative that you combine assignments with clear performance expectations.

Teach new hires the basic tasks of their jobs

This may seem like an obvious step, but many new employees complain that they don't get much guidance in this area. You must remember that it's much harder for them to learn the tasks they need to master than it would be for you or your peers. On-the-job training is essential to effective new employee development. On-the-job training can include providing new employees with job aids, reference manuals, and procedural guides; allowing them to observe more experienced workers; and using mentoring processes. Lead the development of your new employees through formal and informal training as well as coaching with clear performance feedback. Jointly develop a plan to guide their development and direct their learning. Be sure to make efficient use of any spare time your new employees may have by allowing them to learn something new about their jobs.

Help new employees feel a sense of control. For most employees, especially new ones, control is an issue. New employees are frequently assigned tasks and responsibilities without being given any authority. It's not at all uncommon for them to be forced to go through layers and layers of the organization to obtain approvals for even small modifications to job procedures they may feel necessary. Consider whether this is always sound from a business perspective, and allow new employees to have as much personal control as possible. If feasible, give your new employees at least some authority to implement new ideas and methodologies.

Points for Reflection

Do you realize that one of the most important factors in retaining new employees is giving them meaningful and challenging work? Think about the tasks you are assigning to your new employees. Are you making full use of their skills? Would *they* say you are? Have you asked them?

Fourteen

Step 12: Help New Employees Acquire the Necessary Knowledge, Skills, and Abilities

As you are probably well aware, your new hires may lack certain skills that they need to successfully perform their jobs. In fact, you should anticipate this. It's unrealistic for employers to expect new employees, particularly new graduates, to have all the knowledge, skills, and abilities (KSAs) that may be required. Your responsibility as their manager is to identify the competencies needed to complete work tasks and to provide opportunities for your new employees to acquire them.

Most likely, you are responsible for determining the type and level of training your new hires require as well as organizing and directing this training. This is not an obligation that you should take lightly. You must consider a host of factors when making decisions regarding training methodology, including the learners' need to know, readiness to learn, motivation to learn, and prior experiences. Volumes have been written on the subject. For our purposes, however, we will assume that your organization has developed and implemented formal training programs that address at least the basic skills that your new employees must master. You should emphasize the importance of these programs and evaluate your employees' progress. If necessary, allow opportunities for your new employees to attend more specialized training initiatives.

Points for Reflection

Continual learning is a necessity in today's work world. Are you providing all of the training your new employees need to be effective? Are you creating a climate in which development is rewarded? Are you a role model for continual learning and development?

Fifteen

Putting the System Together from the Human Resource Perspective

Complete new employee development systems systematically plan and integrate development experiences in three key areas: orientation, formal training, and formal and informal mentoring and coaching. In addition to development experiences, two other factors—effective supervisors and program evaluation—also serve important roles in new employee development systems.

Orientation

Orientations are important, but they are rarely effective at providing more than a basic introduction to an organization. They deserve lots of attention because they are a new employee's first encounter with their new organization, but too much is often expected of them. Look at orientations as just initial introductions, as a place for new hires to meet the company, and as a place to get started.

Training

Training programs should be an integral part of your employee development process. The overall process should include training programs that teach managers how to develop new employees, new employees how to manage the breaking-in process, and coworkers how to include and support new employees. These training programs should be well coordinated to form a comprehensive training block that covers all facets of new employee development from the new employees', managers', and coworkers' perspectives.

Mentoring and Coaching in the Workplace

Mentoring and coaching are an integral part of the employee development process. Mentors and coaches from within the organization should be assigned or made available to new employees to help ease their transition into their jobs. These coaches should be "seasoned" employees selected for their ability to model desired organizational attitudes and behaviors. Despite their desirable attitudes and behaviors, the employees selected as coaches and mentors must be trained in new employee development. Once trained, they should assume an active role in a new employee's first year on the job. Regular and frequent opportunities for interactions between mentors and new employees should be created.

If at all possible, provide a structured mentoring program. If that's not possible, encourage your new hires to seek out older, more experienced employees who would be willing to help and advise them. As an added benefit, you will find that a mentoring program for your new employees will change the type of interaction you have with these employees. Your conversations will shift from operational issues or the how-to's of their jobs to broader issues such as visioning, making contributions, and adding value.

Effective Supervisors

It almost goes without saying that new employees' supervisors are a critical element of the new employee development team. It is important for them to know how to facilitate learning through training classes and on the job. Your employee development system should have provisions to pair new employees, whenever possible, with supervisors selected for their new employee development skills—that is, supervisors who are particularly proficient at coaching and mentoring, identifying and teaching attitudes for success, demonstrating work savvy, and so on. In addition, supervisors need to be recognized and rewarded for effective new employee development efforts.

Evaluation of Development Programs

New employee development programs should be regularly monitored and evaluated. Periodic evaluations should measure results and serve as a check to see if the programs' goals are being met. Ideally, an employee who has demonstrated the ability to mentor new employees should be assigned the overall responsibility for new employees' development, and development processes should be continuously improved. In addition, the organization should ensure that processes are in place to solve problems that new employees may experience.

Conclusion

New Employee Development Is a Wise Investment

The transition from college to employment is sometimes a difficult one for both new graduates and their employers. Here are some typical comments from managers of new employees and some words of advice:

"They don't seem to fit in"

Integrate new employees immediately. Make sure they know from day one that they are part of the team and you're glad of it. Accept them, include them, and respect them. (Warning: this is easier said than done.) Many times, not fitting in simply means the new employees haven't been integrated well enough yet.

"Isn't our orientation program enough?"

Orientation is important, but it's not enough to enable a new employee to be successful. Develop a breaking-in plan that fits the unique needs of the individual. Design the breaking-in process as carefully as you would any other aspect of your business. Work with each new employee to tailor a plan that fits his or her unique background, interests, and needs.

"They don't act very mature"

Remember what it's like to be new. Make a conscious effort to recall the anxieties, challenges, and frustrations of being a new employee. You'll be amazed at how much you have forgotten. Then, change your approach and manage your new hires as new employees, not experienced ones.

"They aren't 'hitting the ground running'"

Give your new hires time to adapt. New employee development doesn't happen overnight, particularly for recent graduates. Make adaptation time part of the training cycle. It may take recent graduates a while to get up to speed.

"New employees take too much time"

Treat new employee development as a process, not an event. Effective development doesn't happen by "doing a program," writing a manual, or focusing on orientation for just a week or so. It is a process that occurs day by day, week in and week out. It involves everyone in the company, takes time to implement, and can last up to a year—but it pays huge returns!

Good times or bad, large company or small, no one can ever afford to scrimp on new employee development. Tough times make it even more important that every dollar be spent wisely; good times usually mean a tight labor market, so employee retention is vitally important. Successfully implementing a comprehensive system for new employee development can pay huge returns by reducing turnover, increasing productivity, and shortening the learning curve. No business can afford to ignore new employee development. It represents a small incremental investment to ensure that you don't waste the large amounts of money you are investing in new employees.

Index

college versus work, 9–12, 26
communication skills, building,
   39
confidence, 20–21
conformance of new employees,
   31
control, imparting sense of, 63
costs of managing new
   employees, 5–6
culture, organizational, 45–48
culture of college versus work,
   11

D

determining appropriate
   training, 65–66
development programs. See
   new employee development
   system
dues, paying, 54–55

E

effective managers, 58
effective supervisors, 69
employees' readiness for
   learning, 18–19
encouraging new learning,
   18–19
examples, setting, 23, 44, 55
expectations of new employees,
   25–27

F

first impressions, teaching
   importance of, 33–35

first year of work
   versus college, 10
   goals, 12–13
   importance of, 4
fitting in by new employees,
   71–72
followership skills, teaching,
   41–44
fostering good attitudes,
   11–12, 17–24

G

goals, first-year, 12–13
goals of new employee
   development system,
   12–13
Golden Rule, 20

H

hiring recent graduates, 9
humility, 18

I

implementing a new employee
   development system,
   67–70
impression-making skills,
   teaching, 33–35
inappropriate attitudes, 18
insecurity of new employees,
   47
interpersonal-skill-building
   programs, 39
isolation, problems of, 37–38

W

Related Books

How to Succeed in Your First Job: Tips for New College Graduates, Elwood F. Holton III and Sharon S. Naquin

This book teaches new college graduates *what* they need to learn and *how* to learn it. It uses the twelve-part new employee development model to teach recent graduates how to make the transition from college to work. The emphasis is on helping readers learn how college not only fails to fully prepare them for the workplace but also countertrains them so the transition is even more difficult. Readers learn key tasks within the twelve-part model that will help make their transition smoother.

Learning about a new organization is a process that is fundamentally different from learning in a classroom. Even if employees know what to learn, they also need help learning how to learn about the organizations they've just joined. This book first presents an interview protocol that newcomers can use to interview their colleagues and supervisors about topics critical to new employees. Worksheets are also provided to help them analyze the information they collect using the twelve-part new employee development model. At the conclusion, readers develop a personal action and development plan. Analysis sheets offer the perfect tool for new employees and managers to discuss success factors and begin a customized development process for each individual.

So You're New Again: How to Succeed When You Change Jobs, Elwood F. Holton III and Sharon S. Naquin

This book is targeted at new employees with prior work experience who are making significant transitions into new workplaces. These "new" employees could be ones changing companies or ones making significant changes within an organization (e.g., transferring between departments). The twelve-part new employee development model is again used but with a special focus on issues that experienced professionals encounter. Considerable emphasis is placed on the *unlearning* process. For experienced employees, the biggest issues are often not in knowing what to learn but in being able to unlearn and let go of old ways of doing business. Each development task in the twelve-part model teaches them what they must learn *and* what they must unlearn to make a successful transition.

About the Authors

Elwood F. Holton III, Ed.D., is a professor of human resource development (HRD) at Louisiana State University, where he also coordinates the HRD programs and serves as executive director of the Center for Leadership Development. He is also the im-mediate past president of the Academy of Human Resource Development. He consults with public, private, and nonprofit organizations on all types of human resource development, leadership development, and performance improvement projects. Holton has developed and refined his twelve-step model through numerous presentations to new employee and human resource practitioner groups, including consulting engagements in organizations such as J. P. Morgan, Enterprise Rent-A-Car, the U.S. Department of Energy, the U.S. General Services Administration, and the Multiple Sclerosis Society. He is the author of 11 books and more than 150 articles.

Sharon S. Naquin, Ph.D., is the director of the Office of Human Resource Development Research and an assistant professor of human resource development at Louisiana State University. She has eleven years of experience in corporate human resources. In those roles, she has recruited, hired, and trained hundreds of new employees. As a consultant, she has worked on all types of human resource, employee training, and performance improvement problems. She has also published in the areas of dispositional effects on adult learning in the workplace, organizational needs analysis, leadership development, performance improvement systems, community workforce development systems, and management development evaluation.